Writings of John Wesley

Upper Room Spiritual Classics®

Selected, edited, and introduced by
KEITH BEASLEY-TOPLIFFE

UPPER
ROOM BOOKS®
NASHVILLE

WRITINGS OF JOHN WESLEY
Copyright © 1997 by Upper Room Books
Previously published as *A Longing for Holiness: Selected Writings of John Wesley*
All rights reserved.

Upper Room Books˚ website: books.upperroom.org

Cover design: Tim Green | Faceout Studio
Interior design and typesetting: PerfecType, Nashville, TN

ISBN 978-0-8358-1656-4 (print) | ISBN 978-0-8358-1695-3 (mobi) | ISBN 978-0-8358-1696-0 (epub)

Library of Congress Cataloging-in-Publication Data

Wesley, John, 1703–1791.
    [Selections. 1997]
    A longing for holiness: selected writings of John Wesley.
       p.   cm.—(Upper Room spiritual classics. Series 1)
    ISBN 0-8358-0827-0
    1. Christian life—Methodist authors. 2. Holiness—Early works to 1800. 3. Wesley, John, 1703-1791. 4. Methodism. I. Title. II. Series.
BX8217.W54L662 1997
287—dc21   96-52167
                                                                            CIP

Contents

Introduction

Tens of millions of Christians around the world look to John Wesley as the founder (or one of the founders) of their denomination. Assorted Methodists and Wesleyans, Nazarenes, and members of various holiness churches all lay claim to his legacy. Wesley, however, did not intend to found even one denomination. He saw himself as the leader of a revival movement within the Church of England, the overseer of a network of "societies" designed to supplement people's regular church attendance. His hope was "to reform the nation, and especially the church—and to spread scriptural holiness through the land."

Wesley's special genius was to recognize good ideas when he saw them and integrate them into organizational or theological systems. He was not an innovator. Most of the characteristic methods and structures of his societies—subdividing into small groups for mutual nurture (bands and classes), field preaching, using lay preachers, and meeting all the preachers annually in conferences—were found elsewhere or began in individual societies. Wesley recognized their usefulness, refined them, and worked them into his growing institutional system. His theology was grounded in a thorough knowledge of scripture as well as copious reading of ancient, medieval, and modern authors. He tested theological ideas by experience, whether his own or that of others, and he looked always for practical implications and fruits.

Wesley saw the importance of holy living for people at any point in the faith journey. Anyone can benefit from doing good, avoiding evil, and using the means of grace, that is, by developing holy habits. But the grace of the Holy Spirit, he also stressed, is necessary before inward transformation can truly begin. Such transformation continues throughout the Christian's life, and is seen as a process leading toward perfection in love—to loving God with all of one's heart, soul, mind, and strength and loving one's neighbor as oneself. Maintaining this dynamic tension between God's action of grace in the Christian's soul and the Christian's own efforts to live in response to grace formed Wesley's most important theological contribution. This dynamic tension was supported by a second one—between reason (knowing about God) and experience (knowing God personally).

The selections here include excerpts from Wesley's *Journal* that tell of his own struggle to move from knowing about God and being devoted to God to *knowing* God and feeling an assurance of God's love. They continue with a portrait of Christian perfection ("The Character of a Methodist") and practical suggestions for those on the way.

Wesley's World

When Wesley was born in 1703, England was emerging from more than a century and a half of religious conflict. Reforms and counterreforms had created an atmosphere of controversy and even turmoil.

In 1532, King Henry VIII had effected the separation of the Church of England from Roman Catholicism, with himself as head of the church. The new church was heavily influenced by Calvinist and Lutheran Protestantism, although it sought a "middle way" between the most radical reforms and the Catholic tradition. The reforms continued during the reign of Edward VI (1547–53) under the leadership of Archbishop Thomas Cranmer. The first *Book of Common Prayer* was published in 1549. This prayer book (as revised in 1553 and 1662) still formed the basis for public and private worship in the Church of England in Wesley's day.

After Edward's death, his half sister Mary came to the throne and attempted to restore Roman Catholicism. She executed many of the leaders of the English Reformation, including Cranmer. After Mary's death in 1558, her half sister Elizabeth returned England to Protestantism. Her forty-four-year reign gave time for the Church of England to become firmly established.

Elizabeth was succeeded by her cousin James I (reigned 1603–25), who authorized the translation of the Bible into

English (1611) that commonly bears his name. James and his son Charles I (reigned 1625–49) moved slowly but steadily toward Roman Catholicism. The strongly Puritan (Calvinist) Parliament responded by raising its own army to overthrow Charles and execute him. For ten years the English Commonwealth existed without a king and without any established church. Baptists and Quakers were free to exist alongside the Puritans and other Calvinist groups. Then, in 1660, Parliament restored Charles II (the son of Charles I) to the throne, and reestablished the Church of England. Anyone not agreeing to abide by the Book of Common Prayer and other defining documents of the Church of England might be subject to arrest. Among the dissenting or "nonconforming" ministers were John Bunyan, who wrote *The Pilgrim's Progress* (published 1678) while in jail, and Samuel Annesley and John Westley *[sic]*, the grandfathers of John Wesley.

But the time of religious dissension and controversy was not over. James II (reigned 1685–88) openly embraced Roman Catholicism, even though he was officially the Supreme Governor of the Church of England. This strange situation ended when James was deposed in favor of his daughter, Mary II, and her husband, William III of Orange. Their reign began with the Acts of Toleration (1689), which allowed Protestant dissenters freedom to practice their religion as long as both ministers and meetinghouses were registered with the government. Toleration did not extend to Roman Catholics and Unitarians.

One consequence of this history of religious upheaval was a suspicion of any sort of religious fervor. Reasonable religion was the watchword of the day. Deism, which pictured God as aloof and uninvolved with creation, attracted many. Others preached a sort of "justification by sincerity" and saw the essence of Christianity as an earnest effort to do good. This view downplayed a relationship with Christ or an experience of God's love. It was for such a sincere and methodical effort to do good and to live devout, disciplined lives that the Wesleys began the Holy Club (see below).

Meanwhile, another reaction to "reasonable" religion was gaining force in Europe. A movement known as Pietism arose within German Lutheranism in the late-seventeenth century under the leadership of Philipp Jacob Spener. It promoted personal and inward religion in place of intellectualism. It emphasized the heart over the mind and made extensive use of small groups for Bible study and prayer. Similar "religious societies" began in many places in England, including one begun in 1700 by Samuel Wesley, John Wesley's father. Pietism also fueled the spread of a group in Europe known as the Moravians, which in turn spread to America and England and had a profound influence on Wesley.

During Wesley's lifetime, England also underwent profound social upheaval. The Industrial Revolution began, sending the predominantly rural population to the cities, creating overcrowding and poverty. As people migrated from rural parishes, the city churches were unprepared to receive them. These were people ready to hear Wesley or others who would preach to them in fields or coal pits or wherever space could be found.

Wesley's Life

John Wesley was born June 17, 1703, in Epworth, Lincolnshire, England, where his father, Samuel, was rector. John's education began when he was five, primarily under the direction of his mother, Susanna. In 1709, the rectory in Epworth caught fire and John was rescued from an upper-story window shortly before the roof collapsed. Susanna taught him to regard himself as a "brand plucked from the burning," saved by divine providence for some special purpose.

In 1714, Wesley left home for the Charterhouse school in London, then continued his education at Christ Church College, Oxford. At his father's urging, he prepared for ordination. Beginning in 1725, he read a series of books that convinced him of the necessity of devoting his life to God, including *Rules and Exercises of Holy Living and Dying* by Jeremy Taylor, *The Imitation of Christ* by Thomas à Kempis, and *A Serious Call to a Devout and Holy Life* by William Law. Wesley was ordained as a priest in 1728 and served briefly as his father's assistant. He returned to Oxford to serve as a Fellow of Lincoln College, teaching logic, philosophy, and Greek. There he found his younger brother Charles had become serious about religion and gathered a small group of friends. John soon became the leader of this Holy Club. Because of the group's highly structured approach to prayer, spiritual reading, attendance at Communion, and charitable activity they were dubbed "Methodists" by other students.

In 1735, John, Charles, and two others went to the new colony of Georgia in hope of working as missionaries among the Native Americans as well as serving the spiritual needs of the colonists. On the way, Wesley met a group of German Moravians and was impressed with their faith in the face of danger. In Georgia, he organized groups for spiritual nurture and in one of them met a young woman with whom he fell in love. While he tried to decide whether to marry her or cling to the idea that celibacy was necessary for his own spiritual health, she married someone else. Wesley found an excuse to refuse her Communion and her husband and guardian sued. As the suit dragged on, Wesley took the hint and returned to England, convinced he was a total failure. In London, Wesley continued to meet with Moravians in hope of finding a faith that would give him peace and joy in the Lord. He felt that his prayers were answered in a meeting on May 24, 1738. Within a couple of days Charles had a similar experience. The two brothers could now preach from their own experience what they had known (and preached) as theory.

Over the next several years, John and Charles began to travel around England, preaching and establishing groups that became the United Societies, eventually organized into "classes" and "bands": groups for mutual spiritual direction. At the urging of George Whitefield, one of the Oxford Methodists, they began preaching in fields, sometimes to tens of thousands. The movement was torn by controversy over predestination and quietism (an approach to the spiritual life that emphasized mystical passivity). Wesley began to publish carefully edited extracts from his *Journal* to explain his experience and his teaching, as well as numerous tracts and letters arguing various issues. Despite defections over these issues, the Wesleys managed to hold on to a core of followers. The brothers traveled constantly, mainly between London, Bristol, and Newcastle, but with excursions to Wales, Scotland, Ireland, and the rest of England. The movement continued to grow, and new preachers (both clergy and lay, including some women) joined the Wesleys. In addition to the *Journal* and tracts, John Wesley published sermons, hymnals (filled with hymns by Charles), selections from spiritual classics, and even a book of home remedies, *Primitive Physick*. In 1766, followers who had emigrated to America began to organize societies and classes there, and Wesley sent missionaries to oversee their work.

After another confusing and distressing romance, John Wesley finally did marry in 1751. His wife was a widow, Mrs. Mary (Molly) Vazeille, and proved a terrible choice. She did not want to travel with him, and she suspected him of infidelity while he was on the road. After a few years she left him for good, and Wesley gave up hope of reconciliation. She died in 1781.

Wesley died on March 2, 1791, in his room at the Methodist chapel in London. He had preached his last sermon only seven days before, though his voice was barely audible and he had to be supported by two assistants. That did not really matter. He was so revered that people came simply to be in his presence. At the time of his death there were more than 70,000 Methodists in the British Isles and an additional 80,000 in North America.

Further Reading

A new scholarly edition of Wesley's works was published by Abingdon Press. A selection of his writings with extensive introductions is *John Wesley,* edited by Albert C. Outler, from Oxford University Press. Two other books on Wesley, both from Abingdon, are *Reasonable Enthusiast: John Wesley and the Rise of Methodism* by Henry D. Rack and *Wesley and the People Called Methodists* by Richard P. Heitzenrater, both from Abingdon. The latter is intended for more popular reading and contains numerous illustrations and maps. Books that influenced Wesley (and are still available) are *Spiritual Affections* by Jonathan Edwards and the works of Gregory of Nyssa.

Note on the Texts

These selections are intended for devotional reading by individuals or groups. They have been edited for ease of reading. Spelling, punctuation, and grammar have been modernized and some obscure words and phrases translated to current usage. Scripture quotations and paraphrases (indicated in the text by italics) have been conformed where possible to the New Revised Standard Version. Some alterations have been made for the sake of inclusive language.

A Prayer of Submission

From *A Collection of Forms of Prayer*

Wesley's first published work was this collection of prayers for each day of the week, morning and evening, gathered and edited from a variety of sources. It was printed in 1733, before his mission trip to Georgia. This is the prayer for Thursday evening.

To you, O God, Father, Son, and Holy Spirit, my Creator, Redeemer, and Sanctifier, I give up myself entirely. May I no longer serve myself, but you, all the days of my life.

I give you my understanding. May it be my only care to know you, your perfections, your works, and your will. Let all things else be as dross unto me, for the excellency of this knowledge, and let me silence all reasonings against whatsoever you teach me, who can neither deceive nor be deceived.

I give you my will. May I have no will of my own. Whatsoever you will, may I will, and that only. May I will your glory in all things, as you do, and make that my end in every thing. May I ever say with the psalmist, *"Whom have I in heaven but*

you? And there is nothing on earth that I desire other than you"*
May I delight to do your will, O God, and rejoice to accept
it. Whatever threatens me, let me say, "It is the Lord; let him
do what seems good to him." And whatever befalls me, let me
give thanks, since it is your will concerning me.

I give you my affections. Dispose of them all. Be my love,
my fear, my joy; and may nothing have any share in them, but
with respect to you and for your sake. What you love, may I
love; what you hate, may I hate; and that in such measures as
you are pleased to prescribe for me.

I give you my body. May I glorify you with it, and preserve
it holy, fit for you, O God, to dwell in. May I neither indulge
it, nor use too much rigor toward it; but keep it, as far as in me
lies, healthy, vigorous, and active, and fit to do you all manner
of service that you shall call for.

I give you all my worldly goods. May I prize them and use
them only for you. May I faithfully restore to you, in the poor,
all you have entrusted me with, above the necessaries of life;
and be content to part with them too, whenever you, my Lord,
shall require them at my hands.

---

*Italics here and throughout indicate scriptural quotations or allusions.
Where possible, they have been conformed to the New Revised Standard Version.

I give you my credit and reputation. May I never value it, but only in respect of you; nor endeavor to maintain it, but as it may do the service and advance your honor in the world.

I give you myself and my all. Let me look upon myself to be nothing, and to have nothing, apart from you. Be the sole disposer and governor of myself and all; be my portion and my all.

O my God and my all, when hereafter I shall be tempted to break this solemn engagement, when I shall be pressed to conform to the world and to the company and customs that surround me, may my answer be: "I am not my own. I am not for myself, not for the world, but for my God. I will give unto God the things that are God's. God, be merciful to me a sinner."

A Storm at Sea

Journal, January 1736

Wesley is on his way to the colony of Georgia to be a missionary to Native Americans. On the same boat are several German Moravians.

Fri. 23.—In the evening another storm began. In the morning it increased, so that they were forced to let the ship drive. I could not but say to myself, "How is it that you have no faith?" being still unwilling to die. About one in the afternoon, almost as soon as I had stepped out of the great cabin-door, the sea did not break as usual, but came with a full, smooth tide over the side of the ship. I was vaulted over with water in a moment and so stunned that I scarce expected to lift up my head again, till the sea should give up her dead. But thanks be to God, I received no hurt at all. About midnight the storm ceased.

Sun. 25.—At noon our third storm began. At four it was more violent than before. Now, indeed, we could say, *the stormy wind . . . lifted up the waves of the sea. They mounted up to heaven, they went down to the depths.* The winds roared round about us, and (what I never heard before) whistled as distinctly as if it had been a human voice. The ship not only rocked to and fro with the utmost violence, but shook and jarred with such an unequal, grating motion that one could only with great difficulty keep one's hold of any thing, and not stand a moment without it. Every ten minutes came a shock against the stern or side of the ship, which one would think should dash the planks in pieces. At this time a child, privately baptized before, was brought to be received into the church. It put me in mind of Jeremiah's buying the field, when the Chaldeans were put on the point of destroying Jerusalem, and seemed a pledge of the mercy God designed to show us, even in the land of the living.

We spent two or three hours after prayers in conversation suitable to the occasion, confirming one another in a calm submission to the wise, holy, gracious will of God. And now a storm did not appear so terrible as before. Blessed be the God of all consolation!

At seven I went to the Germans. I had long before observed the great seriousness of their behavior. Of their humility they had given a continual proof, by performing those servile tasks for other passengers that none of the English would undertake. For this they desired—and would receive—no pay, saying, "it was good for their proud hearts," and "their loving Savior had done more for them." And every day had given them occasion of showing a meekness which no injury could move. If they were pushed, struck, or thrown down, they rose again and went away; but no complaint was found in their mouth. There was soon an opportunity to test whether they were delivered from the spirit of fear, as well as from that of pride, anger, and revenge. In the midst of the psalm wherewith their service began, the sea broke over, split the mainsail in pieces, covered the ship, and poured in between the decks, as if the great deep had already swallowed us up. A terrible screaming began among the English. The Germans calmly sang on. I asked one of them afterward, "Were you not afraid?" He answered, "I thank God, no." I asked, "But were not your women and children afraid?" He replied, mildly, "No, our women and children are not afraid to die."

From them I went to their crying, trembling neighbors and pointed out to them the difference in the hour of trial between those who fear God and those who do not fear God. At twelve the wind fell. This was the most glorious day that I have yet seen.

Wesley Meets a Moravian Leader

Journal, February 1736

Wesley, now arrived in Georgia, meets A. G. Spangenberg, a leader of the Moravians already in Georgia.

Sat. 7.—Mr. Oglethorpe returned from Savannah with Mr. Spangenberg, one of the pastors of the Germans. I soon found what spirit he was of and asked his advice with regard to my own conduct. He said, "My brother, I must first ask you one or two questions. Have you the witness within yourself? Does the Spirit of God bear witness with your spirit, that you are a child of God?" I was surprised and did not know what to answer. He observed it and asked, "Do you know Jesus Christ?" I paused and said, "I know he is the Savior of the world." "True," he replied; "but do you know that he has saved you?" I answered, "I hope he has died to save me." He only added, "Do you know yourself?" I said, "I do." But I fear they were vain words.

Mon. 9.—I asked him many questions, both concerning himself and the church at Hernhuth. The substance of his answers was this:

"At eighteen years old, I was sent to the university of Jena, where I spent some years in learning languages, and vain philosophy, which I have now long been laboring to forget. Here it pleased God, by some that preached his word with power, to overturn my heart. I immediately threw aside all my learning but what tended to save my soul. I shunned all company and retired to a solitary place, resolving to spend my life there. For three days I had much comfort there; but on the fourth it was all gone. I was amazed, and went for advice to an experienced Christian. When I came to him, I could not speak. But he saw my heart and advised me to go back to my house and follow the business Providence called me to. I went back, but was fit for nothing. I could neither do business nor join in any conversation. All I could say to any one was Yes or No. Many times I could not say even that nor understand the plainest thing that was said to me. My friends and acquaintances looked upon me as dead, came no more to me, nor spoke about me.

"When I grew better, I began teaching some poor children. Others joining with me, we taught more and more, till there were more than thirty teachers and more than two hundred scholars. I now had invitations to other universities. But I could not accept any, desiring only, if it were the will of God, to be little and unknown. I had spent some years thus, when Professor Breithaupt, of Halle, died. Being then pressed to go there, I believed it was the call of God and went. I had not been long there before many faults were found, both with my behavior and preaching; and offenses increased more and more, till, after half a year, a petition against me was sent to the King of Prussia, who sent an order to the commander at Halle; as a result I was warned to leave the city in forty-eight hours. I did so, and retired to Hernhuth to Count Zinzendorf.

"The village of Hernhuth contains about a thousand souls gathered out of many nations. They hold fast the discipline, as well as the faith and practice, of the apostolic church. Last year the brethren there wanted me to conduct sixteen of them to Georgia, where two lots of ground are assigned us; and with them I have stayed ever since."

I asked where he was to go next. He said, "I have thoughts of going to Pennsylvania. But what God will do with me I do not know. I am blind. I am a child. My Father knows, and I am ready to go wherever he calls."

"Who Shall Convert Me?"

Journal, January 1738

Wesley returned to England feeling himself a thorough failure. He had converted no Native Americans and had been involved in a disastrous romance that led to a lawsuit that drove him from Georgia. As his ship neared England he was certainly at a low point in his life.

On Monday, [January] 9, and the following days, I reflected much on that vain desire, which had pursued me for so many years, of being in solitude, in order to be a Christian. I have now, thought I, solitude enough. But am I, therefore, the nearer being a Christian? Not if Jesus Christ be the model of Christianity. I suspect, indeed, I am much nearer that mystery of Satan, which some writers affect to call by that name. So near that I had probably sunk wholly into it, had not the great mercy of God just now thrown me upon reading Saint Cyprian's works.

Fri. 13.—We had a violent storm, which obliged us to shut all the hatches; the sea was breaking over the ship continually. I was at first afraid, but cried to God and was strengthened.

Before ten I lay down, I bless God, without fear. About midnight we were awakened by a confused noise of seas and wind and men's voices, the like to which I had never heard before. I can compare the sound of the sea breaking over and against the sides of the ship to nothing but large cannon or American thunder. The rebounding, starting, quivering motion of the ship much resembled what is said of earthquakes. The captain was upon deck in an instant. But his men could not hear what he said. It blew a true hurricane, which beginning at southwest, then went west, northwest, north, and in a quarter of an hour, round by the east to the southwest point again. At the same time, because the sea was running (as they term it) mountain-high, and that from many different points at once, the ship would not obey the helm; nor indeed could the steersman, through the violent rain, see the compass. So he was forced to let her run before the wind, and in half an hour the stress of the storm was over.

About noon the next day it ceased. But first I had resolved, God being my helper, not only to preach it to all, but to apply the word of God to every single soul in the ship. If but one, yea, if not one of them will hear, I know my *labor is not in vain.*

I no sooner executed this resolution than my spirit revived. So that from this day I had no more of that fearfulness and heaviness that before almost continually weighed me down. I am sensible that one who sees being "in hell" as an indispensable preparative for being a Christian would say, I had better have continued in that state; and that this unseasonable relief was a curse, not a blessing. But who are you, O man, who, in favor of a wretched hypothesis, thus blaspheme the good gift of God? Has not God himself said, *"To . . . find enjoyment in their toil—this is the gift of God"*? Yea, God sets his own seal to their weak endeavors, while he thus *keeps them occupied with the joy of their hearts.*

Tues. 24.—We spoke with two ships, outward-bound, from whom we had the welcome news of our being but one hundred and sixty leagues from Land's end. My mind was now full of thought; part of which I wrote down as follows:

"I went to America, to convert the Indians. But oh! who shall convert me? Who, what is he that will deliver me from this evil heart of unbelief? I have a fair summer religion. I can talk well; nay, and believe myself while no danger is near: But let death look me in the face and my spirit is troubled. Nor can I say, *'Dying is gain!'"*

> I have a sin of fear, that when I've spun
> My last thread, I shall perish on the shore.

"I think, truly, if the gospel be true, I am safe; for I not only have given, and do give, all my goods to feed the poor; I not only give my body to be burned, drowned, or whatever God shall appoint for me; but I follow after charity—though not as I ought, yet as I can—if haply I may attain it. I *now* believe the gospel is true. I show my faith by my works, by staking my all upon it. I would do so again and again a thousand times, if the choice were still to make. Whoever sees me sees I would be Christian. Therefore are my ways not like others' ways. Therefore I have been, I am, I am content to be, *a by-word and a proverb* of reproach. But in a storm I think, 'What if the gospel be not true? Then you are of all people most foolish. For what have you given your goods, your ease, your friends, your reputation, your country, your life? For what are you wandering over the face of the earth? A dream, *a cleverly devised myth.*' Oh! *Who will rescue me from this body of death?* What shall I do? *"Where shall I fly* from it? Should I fight against it by thinking, or by not thinking of it? A wise man advised me some time since, 'Be still, and go on.' Perhaps this is best, to look upon it as my cross; when it comes, to let it humble me and quicken all my good resolutions, especially that of praying without ceasing; and at other times, to take no thought about it, but quietly to go on *in the work of the Lord."*

"What Have I Learned of Myself?"

Journal, February 1738

After his ship landed, Wesley summarized his trip and what he had learned

It is now two years and almost four months since I left my native country, in order to teach the Georgian Indians the nature of Christianity. But what have I learned myself in the meantime? Why, (what I the least of all suspected) that I who went to America to convert others was never myself converted to God. *I am not out of my mind,* though I thus speak, *but I speak the sober truth.* Perhaps some of those who still dream may awake, and see that as I am, so are they.

Are they read in philosophy? So was I. In ancient or modern tongues? So was I also. Are they versed in the science of divinity? I too have studied it many years. Can they talk fluently about spiritual things? The very same could I do. Are they plenteous in alms? Behold, I gave all my goods to feed the poor. Do they give of their labor as well as of their substance? I have labored more abundantly than they all. Are they willing to suffer for their brethren? I have thrown up my friends, reputation, ease, country; I have put my life in my hand, wandering into strange lands; I have given my body to be devoured by the deep, parched up with heat, consumed by toil and weariness, or whatsoever God should please to bring upon me. But does all this (be it more or less, it does not matter) make me acceptable to God? Does all I ever did or can know, say, give, do, or suffer, justify me in his sight? Yea, or the constant use of all the means of grace? (Which, nevertheless, is meet, right, and our bounden duty.) Or that I know nothing of myself? That I am, as touching outward, moral righteousness blameless? Or (to come closer yet) that I have a rational conviction of all the truths of Christianity? Does all this give me a claim to the holy, heavenly, divine character of a Christian? By no means. If the Oracles of God are true, all these things, though when ennobled by faith in Christ are holy and just and good, yet without it they are dross, fit only to be purged away by the unquenchable fire.

This, then, have I learned in the ends of the earth:

That I have *fallen short of the glory of God.*

That my whole heart is altogether *corrupt and abominable,* and consequently so is my whole life (since it cannot be that a *bad tree* should *bear good fruit).*

That *alienated as* I am *from the life of God,* I am a *child of wrath,* an heir of hell.

That my own works, my own sufferings, my own righteousness, are so far from reconciling me to an offended God, so far from making any atonement for the least of those sins, which are *more in number than the hairs of my head,* that the most specious of them need an atonement themselves, or they cannot abide his righteous judgment.

That *having the sentence of death* in my heart, and having nothing in or of myself to plead, I have no hope but that of being justified freely, *through the redemption that is in Jesus.* I have no hope but that if I seek I shall find Christ, *and be found in him, not having a righteousness of my own that comes from the law, but one that comes through faith in Christ, the righteousness from God based on faith.*

If it be said that I have faith (for many such things have I heard, from many miserable comforters), I answer, so have the devils—a sort of faith. But still they are strangers to the covenant of promise. So the apostles have even at Cana in Galilee, when Jesus first *revealed his glory.* Even then they, in a way, *believed in him.* But they had not then the *faith that conquers the world.* The faith I want is, "a sure trust and confidence in God, that, through the merits of Christ, my sins are forgiven and I am reconciled to the favor of God." I want that faith that Saint Paul recommends to all the world: that faith that enables every one that has it to cry out, *"It is no longer I who live, but it is Christ who lives in me. And the life I now live in the flesh I live by faith in the Son of God, who loved me and gave himself for me."* I want that faith that none can have without knowing that they have it (though many imagine they have it, who do not). For those who have it are *freed from sin*. The whole *body of sin is destroyed* in them. They are freed from fear, having *peace with God through Christ* and boasting in *hope of sharing the glory of God*. And they are freed from doubt *because God's love has been poured into their hearts through the Holy Spirit that has been given to them*, which *Spirit bears witness with their spirit that they are children of God*.

"Preach Faith Till You Have It"

Journal, March and April 1738

Back in England, Wesley met often with Peter Böhler, another German Moravian. Here are accounts of two such meetings.

Sat. March 4.—I found my brother at Oxford, recovering from his pleurisy, and with him Peter Böhler, by whom (in the hand of the great God) I was, on Sunday, the fifth, clearly convinced of unbelief, of the want of that faith whereby alone we are saved.

Immediately it struck into my mind, "Leave off preaching. How can you preach to others, when you have not faith yourself?" I asked Böhler whether he thought I should leave it off or not. He answered, "By no means." I asked, "But what can I preach?" He said, "Preach faith *till* you have it; and then, *because you* have it, you *will* preach faith."

Sat. April 22.—I met Peter Böhler once more. I had now no objection to what he said of the nature of faith; namely, that it is (to use the words of our church) "a sure trust and confidence that a man has in God, that through the merits of Christ his sins are forgiven, and he reconciled to the favor of God." Neither could I deny either the happiness of holiness which he described, as fruits of this living faith. *That very Spirit bears witness with our spirit that we are the children of God,* and *Those who believe have the testimony in their hearts* fully convinced me of the former, as *Those who have been born of God do not sin,* and *Everyone who believes has been born of God* did of the latter. But I could not comprehend what he said about an *instantaneous work.* I could not understand how this faith should be given in a moment, how a man could *at once* be thus turned from darkness to light, from sin and misery to righteousness and joy in the Holy Spirit. I searched the Scriptures again, concerning this very thing, particularly the Acts of the Apostles. But to my utter astonishment, I found scarce an instance there of other than *instantaneous* conversions; scarce any so slow as that of Saint Paul, who was three days in the pangs of the new birth. I had but one retreat left; namely, "God worked in this way in the *first* ages of Christianity, but the times are changed. What reason have I to believe he works in the same manner now? "

But on Sunday, 23, I was beat out of this retreat, too, by the concurring evidence of several living witnesses who testified God had thus worked in themselves, giving them in a moment such a faith in the blood of his Son as translated them out of darkness into light, out of sin and fear into holiness and happiness. Here ended my disputing. I could now only cry out, *"Lord, help my unbelief."*

I asked P. Böhler again whether I ought not to refrain from teaching others. He said, "No, do not hide in the earth the talent God has given you."

A Heart Strangely Warmed

Journal, May 1738

On May 24, 1738, Wesley received the assurance of faith he had been seeking. The moment was so important to him that he inserted a lengthy spiritual autobiography at this point in his journal, with eighteen points. This selection picks up at point 11, which recounts Wesley's return to England from Georgia.

11. On my return to England, January, 1738, being in imminent danger of death and very uneasy on that account, I was strongly convinced that the cause of that uneasiness was unbelief and that the gaining of a true, living faith was the "one thing lacking" for me. But still I did not fix this faith on its right object. I meant only faith in God, not faith in or through Christ. Again, I did not know that I was wholly void of this faith, but only thought that I did not have enough of it. So when Peter Böhler, whom God prepared for me as soon as I came to London, affirmed of true faith in Christ (which is but one) that it had those two fruits inseparably attending it, "dominion over sin, and constant peace coming from a sense of forgiveness," I was quite amazed and looked upon it as a new

gospel. If this was so, it was clear I did not have faith. But I was not willing to be convinced of this. Therefore, I disputed with all my might, and labored to prove that faith might be where these were not, especially where the sense of forgiveness was not. For all the Scriptures relating to this I had been long since taught to interpret differently. Besides, I well saw that no one could, in the nature of things, have such a sense of forgiveness, and not feel it. But I did not *feel* it. If then there was no faith without this, all my pretensions to faith dropped at once.

12. When I met Peter Böhler again, he consented to focus the discussion on the issue that I desired, namely, Scripture and experience. I first consulted the Scripture. But when I set aside the glosses of men and simply considered the words of God, comparing them together, endeavoring to illustrate the obscure by the plainer passages, I found they all worked against me. I was forced to retreat to my last hold: that experience would never agree with the *literal interpretation* of those scriptures, nor could I admit it to be true till I found some living witnesses of it. Accordingly, the next day he came again with three others, all of whom testified of their own personal experience that a true living faith in Christ is inseparable from a sense of pardon for all past—and freedom from all present— sins. They added with one mouth that this faith was the gift, the free gift of God; and that he would surely bestow it upon every soul who earnestly and perseveringly sought it. I was now thoroughly convinced. By the grace of God, I resolved to seek

it unto the end: 1. By absolutely renouncing all dependence, in whole or in part, upon *my own* works or righteousness; on which I had really grounded my hope of salvation, though I did not know it, from my youth up. 2. By adding to the constant use of all the other means of grace, continual prayer for this very thing—justifying, saving faith, a full reliance on the blood of Christ shed for *me,* a trust in him, as *my* Christ, as *my* sole justification, sanctification, and redemption.

13. I continued thus to seek it (though with strange indifference, dullness, and coldness, and unusually frequent relapses into sin) till Wednesday, May 24. I think it was about five this morning, that I opened my Testament on those words, *He has given us . . . his precious and very great promises, so that through them you may . . . become participants of the divine nature.* Just as I went out, I opened it again on those words, *You are not far from the kingdom of God.* In the afternoon I was asked to go to St. Paul's. The anthem was, *Out of the depths I cry to you, O LORD. Lord, hear my voice! Let your ears be attentive to the voice of my supplications! If you, O LORD, should mark iniquities, Lord, who could stand? But there is forgiveness with you, so that you may be revered. . . . O Israel, hope in the LORD! For with the Lord there is steadfast love, and with him is great power to redeem. It is he who will redeem Israel from all its iniquities.*

14. In the evening I went very unwillingly to a society at Aldersgate Street, where one was reading Luther's preface to the Epistle to the Romans. About a quarter before nine, while

he was describing the change that God works in the heart through faith in Christ, I felt my heart strangely warmed. I felt I did trust in Christ, Christ alone for salvation. And an assurance was given me that he had taken away *my* sins, even *mine,* and saved *me* from the law of sin and death.

I began to pray with all my might for those who had in a special way despitefully used me and persecuted me. I then testified openly to all there, what I now first felt in my heart. But it was not long before the enemy suggested, "This cannot be faith, for where is your joy?" Then was I taught that peace and victory over sin are essential to faith in the Captain of our salvation. But, as to the transports of joy that usually attend the beginning of it, especially in those who have mourned deeply, God sometimes gives, sometimes withholds them, according to the counsels of his own will.

After my return home, I was much buffeted with temptations, but cried out, and they fled away. They returned again and again. As often as they returned, I lifted up my eyes and God *sent me help from the sanctuary.* And here I found the chief difference between this and my former state. I was striving, yea, fighting with all my might under the law, as well as under grace. But then I was sometimes, if not often, conquered. Now, I was always conqueror.

Thur. 25.—The moment I awaked, "Jesus, Master," was in my heart and in my mouth; and I found all my strength lay in keeping my eye fixed upon him, and my soul waiting on him continually. Being again at Saint Paul's in the afternoon, I could taste the good word of God in the anthem, which began, "My song shall be always of the loving kindness of the Lord: With my mouth will I ever be showing forth your truth from one generation to another." Yet the enemy injected a fear, "If you do believe, why is there not a more sensible change?" I answered (yet not I), "That I do not know. But this I know, I now have *peace with God*. And I do not sin today, and Jesus my Master has forbid me to take thought for the morrow."

18. "But is not any sort of fear," continued the tempter, "a proof that you do not believe?" I desired my Master to answer for me; and opened his Book upon those words of Saint Paul, *disputes without, fears within*. Then, inferred I, well may fears be within me, but I must go on and tread them under my feet.

"The Christianity That I Teach"

From "The Character of a Methodist"

In 1739, Wesley published this tract on what a Methodist seeks to be.

Methodists are those who had *God's love poured into their hearts through the Holy Spirit that has been given to them, who love the Lord their God with all their hearts, and with all their souls, and with all their minds, and with all their strength.* God is the joy of their hearts, and the desire of their souls; which constantly cry out, *Whom have I in heaven but you? And there is nothing on earth that I desire other than you!* My God and my all! You are *the strength of my heart, and my portion for ever!*

They are therefore happy in God, yea, always happy, as having in them *a spring of water gushing up to eternal life,* and overflowing their souls with peace and joy. *Perfect love* having now *cast out fear,* they *rejoice in the Lord always,* even in *God their Savior.* Having found *redemption through his blood, the forgiveness of their trespasses,* they cannot but rejoice, whenever they look back on the horrible pit out of which they are delivered. They cannot but rejoice, whenever they look on the state wherein they now are: *justified by God's grace as a gift,* and having *peace with God through our Lord Jesus Christ.* For *those who believe have the testimony of this in their hearts,* being now the children of God by faith. *Because they are children, God has sent the Spirit of his Son into their hearts, crying, "Abba, Father!"* And *that very Spirit bears witness with their spirits, that they are children of God.* They rejoice also, whenever they look forward, *in hope of the glory that shall be revealed.* All their bones cry out, *"Blessed be the God and Father of our Lord Jesus Christ! By his great mercy he has given us a new birth into a living hope . . . into an inheritance that is imperishable, undefiled, and unfading, kept in heaven for [us!]"*

And those who have this hope *give thanks in all circumstances* as knowing that this (whatsoever it is) *is the will of God in Christ Jesus for them.* From God, therefore, they cheerfully receive all, saying, "Good is the will of the Lord"; and whether the Lord gives or takes away, equally *blessing the name of the Lord.* For they *have learned to be content with whatever they have.* Whether in ease or pain, whether in sickness or health, whether in life or death, they give thanks from the ground of their hearts to God who orders it for good; knowing that as *every good gift is from above,* so nothing but good can come from the Father of lights, into whose hand they wholly committed their bodies and souls. They cast all their care on him that cares for them, and in everything resting on him, after *making their requests known to God with thanksgiving.*

For indeed they *pray without ceasing.* Not that they are always in the house of prayer; though they neglect no opportunity of being there. Neither are they always on their knees, although they often are, or on their face, before the Lord their God. Nor yet are they always crying aloud to God, for many times *the Spirit intercedes with sighs too deep for words.* Their heart is ever lifted up to God, at all times and in all places. In this they are never hindered, much less interrupted, by any person or thing. In retirement or company, in leisure, business, or conversation, God is in all their thoughts; they walk with God continually, having the loving eye of their minds still fixed upon him, and everywhere seeing him that is invisible.

And while they thus always exercise their love to God, by praying without ceasing, rejoicing evermore, and in everything giving thanks, this commandment is written in their heart, *Those who love God must love their brothers and sisters also.* And they accordingly love their neighbor as themselves. Their hearts are full of love to all humankind. That someone is not personally known to them is no bar to their love; no, nor that someone is known to be such as they approve not, who repays hatred for good will. For they *love their enemies,* yea, and the enemies of God, *the ungrateful and the wicked.* And if it be not in their power *to do good to those who hate them,* yet they cease not to pray for them, though they continue to spurn their love and still *abuse them* and persecute them.

For they are *pure in heart.* The love of God has purified their heart from all revengeful passions, from envy, malice, and wrath, from every unkind temper or malign affection. It has cleansed them from pride and haughtiness of spirit, from which alone comes contention. They have now *clothed themselves with compassion, kindness, humility, meekness, and patience* so that they *bear with and forgive each other, just as the Lord has forgiven them.* And indeed all possible ground for contention is utterly cut off. For none can take from them what they desire; seeing they *do not love the world or the things in the world,* being now *crucified to the world, and the world crucified to them.* God's *name and renown are their soul's desire.*

Agreeable to this one desire is the one design of their life, namely, *not to do their own will, but the will of him that sent them.* They have a single eye. Indeed, where the loving eye of the soul is continually fixed upon God, there can be no darkness at all. All that is in the soul is holiness to the Lord. There is not a motion in their hearts, but is according to God's will. Every thought that arises points to God, and is in obedience to the law of Christ.

And *the tree is known by its fruits.* For as they love God, so they keep his commandments; not only some, or most of them, but all, from the least to the greatest. Whatever God has forbidden, they avoid; whatever God has enjoined, they do, whether it be little or great, hard or easy, joyous or grievous to the flesh. It is their glory so to do. It is their daily crown of rejoicing, *to do the will of God on earth, as it is in heaven.* For their obedience is in proportion to their love for the source from whence it flows. And therefore, loving God with all their hearts, they serve God with all their strength. They continually present their souls and bodies *a living sacrifice, holy and acceptable to God.* All the talents they have received they employ according to their Master's will; every power and faculty of the soul, every member of the body.

By consequence, whatsoever they do is all to the glory of God. In all their employments of every kind, they not only aim at this (which is implied in having a single eye), but they actually attain it. Their business and refreshments, as well as their prayers, all serve this great end, to advance the glory of God, by peace and good will among people. Their one invariable rule is this: *whatever you do, in word or deed, do everything in the name of the Lord Jesus, giving thanks to God the Father through him.*

Nor do the customs of the world at all hinder their *running the race that is set before them.* They know that vice does not lose its nature, though it becomes ever so fashionable; and they remember that *each will be accountable to God.* They cannot, therefore, *follow even a majority in wrongdoing.* They cannot *feast sumptuously every day,* or *store up for themselves treasures on earth.* They cannot *adorn themselves* on any pretense with *gold ornaments or fine clothing.* They cannot *speak evil* of their neighbors, any more than they can either for God or any person. They cannot utter an unkind word of any one, for love keeps the door of their lips. But *whatever is pure, whatever is pleasing, whatever is* justly *commendable,* they think and speak and act.

Lastly, as they have time, they *work for the good of all,* neighbors and strangers, friends and enemies: not only to their bodies, by *feeding the hungry, clothing the naked, visiting those that are sick or in prison;* but much more to their souls, to awaken those that sleep in death; to bring those who are awakened to the atoning blood, and to provoke those who have peace with God to abound more in love and in good works. And they are willing to *spend and be spent* herein, so they may *all come to the measure of the full stature of Christ.*

These are the principles and practices of our sect; these are the marks of a true Methodist. Someone may say, "Why, these are only the common, fundamental principles of Christianity!" As you have said, so I mean. This is the very truth. I know they are no other. And I would to God both you and all people knew that I, and all who follow my judgment, do vehemently refuse to be distinguished from others by any but the common principles of Christianity—the plain old Christianity that I teach, renouncing and detesting all other marks of distinction. And whoever are what I preach (let them be called what they will, for names do not change the nature of things) are Christians, not in name only, but in heart and in life. By these marks, by these fruits of a living faith, do we labor to distinguish ourselves from the unbelieving world, from all those whose minds or lives are not according to the gospel of Christ. But from real Christians, of whatsoever denomination they be, we earnestly desire not to be distinguished at all, not from any who sincerely follow after what they know they have not yet attained. *Whoever does the will of my Father in heaven is my brother and sister and mother.* Is your heart right, as my heart is with yours? I ask no further question. If it be, give me your hand.

How We Are to Live

"The Rules of the United Societies"

The ideal portrait of a Methodist was worked out in practice through participation in the United Societies. These rules, created in 1739 and published after considerable refinement in 1743, set the standard for members in the Societies.

In the latter end of the year 1739, eight or ten persons came to me in London, who appeared to be deeply convinced of sin, and earnestly groaning for redemption. They desired (as did two or three more the next day) that I would spend some time with them in prayer and advise them how to flee from the wrath to come, which they saw continually hanging over their heads. That we might have more time for this great work, I appointed a day when they might all come together, which from thenceforward they did every week on Thursday in the evening. To these, and as many more as desired to join with them (for their number increased daily) I gave such advice from time to time that I judged most needful for them; and we always concluded our meeting with prayer suited to various needs.

This was the rise of the United Society, first at London and then in other places. Such a society is no other than a company of persons having the form and seeking the power of godliness, united in order to pray together, to receive the word of exhortation, and to watch over one another in love that they may help each other to work out their salvation.

That it may the more easily be discerned whether they are indeed working out their own salvation, each society is divided into smaller companies called "classes," according to their respective places of abode. There are about twelve persons in every class, one of whom is styled the leader. It is the business of the leaders:

(1) To see each person in his class once a week at least, in order to inquire how their souls fare; to advise, reprove, comfort, or exhort, as occasion may require; to receive what they are willing to give toward the relief of the poor;

(2) To meet the minister and the stewards of the society once a week; to pay to the stewards what they have received of their several classes in the week preceding; and to show their account of what each person has contributed.

There is one only condition previously required in those who desire admission into these societies—"a desire to *flee from the wrath to come,* to be saved from their sins." But wherever this is really fixed in the soul, it will be shown by its fruits. It is therefore expected of all who continue therein, that they should continue to evidence their desire of salvation:

First, by doing no harm, by avoiding evil of every kind; especially that which is most generally practiced. Such as the taking the name of God in vain;

the profaning the day of the Lord, either by doing ordinary work thereon, or by buying or selling;

drunkenness, buying or selling spirituous liquors, or drinking them, unless in cases of extreme necessity;

fighting, quarreling, brawling; going to court;

returning evil for evil, or railing for railing;

using many words in buying or selling;

buying or selling uncustomed [i.e., smuggled] goods;

giving or taking things on usury;

uncharitable or unprofitable conversations;

doing to others as we would not have them do unto us;

doing what we know is not for the glory of God, as the putting on of gold or costly apparel;

taking such diversions as cannot be used in the name of the Lord Jesus; singing those songs or reading those books which do not tend to the knowledge or love of God;

softness and needless self-indulgence;

laying up treasures upon earth.

It is expected of all who continue in these societies, that they should continue to evidence their desire of salvation, second, by doing good, by being in every way as merciful as they can be:

as they have opportunity, doing good of every possible sort, and as far as is possible, to all: to their bodies, according to the

ability that God gives, by giving food to the hungry, by clothing the naked, by visiting or helping them that are sick, or in
prison; and to their souls, by instructing, reproving, or exhort-
ing all they have any contact with;

trampling underfoot that enthusiastic doctrine of devils,
that "we are not to do good unless our heart be free to it";

by doing good, especially to them that are of the household
of faith, or groaning so to be, employing them preferably to
others, buying from one another, helping each other in business (and all the more so, because the world will love its own,
and them only);

by all possible diligence and frugality, that the gospel be
not blamed;

by running with patience the race that is set before them,
denying themselves and taking up their cross daily;

submitting to bear the reproach of Christ, to be as the filth
and offscouring of the world;

and expecting that others *should say all kinds of evil against
them falsely for the Lord's sake.*

It is expected of all who desire to continue in these societies
that they should continue to evidence their desire of salvation,
third, by attending upon all the ordinances of God. Such are
the public worship of God; the ministry of the word, either
read or expounded; the supper of the Lord; private prayer;
searching the Scriptures; and fasting, or abstinence.

These are the General Rules of our societies, all of which we are taught by God to observe, even in his written word—the only rule, and the sufficient rule, both of our faith and practice. And all these, we know his Spirit writes on every truly awakened heart. If there be any among us who do not observe them, who habitually break any of them, let it be made known unto the one who watches over those souls as one that must give account. I will admonish such of the error of their ways. I will bear with them for a season. But if they do not repent, they have no more place among us. We have delivered our own souls.

How We Are to Give

From "The Use of Money"

The text for this sermon is Luke 16:9: "Make to yourselves friends of the mammon of unrighteousness, that, when ye fail, they may receive you into everlasting habitations" (KJV). NRSV has "Make friends for yourselves by means of dishonest wealth so that when it is gone, they may welcome you into the eternal homes," which is not amenable to Wesley's interpretation. Wesley's first two points were "Gain all you can," and "Save all you can." This selection is the final point.

But let not any imagine that they have done anything by going only thus far, by "gaining and saving all they can," if they were to stop here. All this is nothing if they go not forward, if they do not point all this at a further end. Nor, indeed, can people properly be said to save anything, if they only lay it up. You may as well throw your money into the sea as bury it in the earth. And you may as well bury it in the earth as in your chest, or in the bank of England. Not to use is effectually to throw it away. If, therefore, you would indeed *make yourselves friends of the mammon of unrighteousness,* add the third rule to the two preceding. Having first gained all you can, and secondly saved all you can, then give all you can.

In order to see the ground and reason of this, consider: When the Possessor of heaven and earth brought you into being and placed you in this world, he placed you here not as a proprietor, but a steward; as such he entrusted you for a season with goods of various kinds, but the sole ownership of these still rests in God, nor can ever be alienated from him. As you yourself are not your own, but God's, such is likewise all that you enjoy. Such is your soul and your body, not your own, but God's. And so is your substance in particular. God has told you in the most clear and express terms how you are to employ it for him: in such a manner that it may be all a holy sacrifice, acceptable through Christ Jesus. And this light, easy service he has promised to reward with an eternal weight of glory.

The directions God has given us, concerning the use of our worldly substance may be comprised in the following particulars. If you desire to be a faithful and a wise steward, out of that portion of your Lord's goods, which he has for the present lodged in your hands, but with the right of resuming whenever it pleases him, first, provide things needful for yourself: food to eat, raiment to put on, whatever nature moderately requires for preserving the body in health and strength. Second, provide these for your family or any others who pertain to your household. If, when this is done, there be a surplus left, then do good *for those of the family of faith.* If there be a surplus still, *whenever you have an opportunity, work for the good of all.* In so doing, you give all you can; nay, in a real sense, all you have. For all that is laid out in this manner is really given to God. You *give to God the things that are God's,* not only by what you give to the poor, but also by what you spend in providing things needful for yourself and your household.

If then a doubt should at any time arise in your mind concerning what you are going to spend, either on yourself or any part of your family, you have an easy way to remove it. Calmly and seriously inquire,

1. In expending this, am I acting according to my character? Am I acting herein, not as a proprietor, but as a steward of my Lord's goods?

2. Am I doing this in obedience to his word? In what scripture does he require me so to do?

3. Can I offer up this action, this expense, as a sacrifice to God through Jesus Christ?

4. Have I reason to believe that for this very work I shall have a reward at the resurrection of the just?

You will seldom need anything more to remove any doubt that arises on this head; but, by this fourfold consideration, you will receive clear light as to the way you should go.

If any doubt still remain, you may further examine yourself by prayer, according to those categories of inquiry. Try whether you can say to the Searcher of hearts, your conscience not condemning you, "Lord, you see I am going to expend this sum on that food, apparel, furniture. And you know, I act therein with a single eye, as a steward of your goods, expending this portion of them thus, in pursuance of the design you had in entrusting me with them. You know I do this in obedience to your word, as you command it. Let this, I beseech you, be a holy sacrifice, acceptable though Jesus Christ! And give me a witness in myself, that for this labor of love I shall have a recompense, when you reward everyone according to their works." Now if your conscience bear you witness in the Holy Spirit that this prayer is well pleasing to God, then you have no reason to doubt whether the expense is right and good and such as will never make you ashamed.

You see, then, what it is to *make yourselves friends of the mammon of unrighteousness,* and by what means you may procure that when you are gone, *they may welcome you into the eternal homes.* You see the nature and extent of truly Christian prudence, so far as it relates to the use of that great talent, money. Gain all you can without hurting either yourself or your neighbor in soul or body, by applying yourself to this with uninterrupted diligence and with all the understanding that God has given you. Save all you can, by cutting off every expense that serves only to indulge foolish desire, to gratify either the desire of the flesh, the desire of the eye, or the pride of life; waste nothing, living or dying, on sin or folly, whether on yourself or your children. And then, give all you can, or in other words, give all you have to God. Do not stint to this or that proportion. Give to God not a tenth, not a third, not half, but all that is God's, be it more or less. Give by employing all, on yourself, your household, the household of faith, and all humankind in such manner that you may give a good account of your stewardship, when you can be no longer stewards. Give in such a manner as the oracles of God direct, both by general and particular precepts. Give in such a manner that whatever you do may be *an offering of pleasing odor to God,* and that every act may be rewarded in that day, when the Lord comes with all his saints.

Advice about Pride

From *A Plain Account of Christian Perfection*

A key emphasis in Wesley's teaching was that believers could go on to perfection in love and, indeed, were supposed to do so. Various writings on the subject were gathered together in the short book A Plain Account of Christian Perfection *published in 1767, including a selection from "The Character of a Methodist," which Wesley calls "the first tract I ever wrote expressly on this subject." Toward the end of the book, Wesley offers advice to those who have progressed far in the Christian life, taken from a tract first published in 1762. First, advice about pride.*

Watch and pray continually against pride. If God has cast it out, see that it enter no more. It is fully as dangerous as desire, and you may slide back into it unawares, especially if you think there is no danger of it. "Nay, but I ascribe all I have to God." So you may, and be proud nevertheless. For it was pride, not only to ascribe anything we have to ourselves, but to think we have what we really have not. Mr. [William] Law, for instance, ascribed all the light he had to God, and so far he was humble. But then he thought he had more light than any man living;

and this was palpable pride. So you ascribe all the knowledge you have to God, and in this respect you are humble. But if you think you have more than you really have, or if you think you are so taught of God as no longer to need human teaching, pride lies at the door. Yes, you have need to be taught, not only by Mr. Morgan, by one another, by Mr. Maxfield, or by me, but by the weakest preacher in London; yea, by all people. For God sends by whom God will send.

Do not therefore say to any who would advise or reprove you, "You are blind; you cannot teach me." Do not say, "This is your wisdom, your carnal reason." But calmly weigh the thing before God.

Always remember, much grace does not always imply much light. These do not always go together. As there may be much light where there is but little love, so there may be much love where there is little light. The heart has more heat than the eye. Yet it cannot see. God has wisely arranged the members of the body that none may say to another, *"I have no need of you."*

To imagine none can teach you but those who are themselves saved from sin is a very great and dangerous mistake. Give no place to it for a moment: it would lead you into a thousand other mistakes, and that irrecoverably. Obey and *respect those who have charge of you in the Lord,* and do not think you know better than they. Know their place and your own, always remembering that much love does not imply much light.

Not observing this has led some into many mistakes and into at least the appearance of pride. Oh, beware of the appearance and the thing! *Let the same mind be in you that was in Christ Jesus.* And *clothe yourselves with humility.* Let it not only fill, but cover you all over. Let modesty and self-diffidence appear in all your words and actions. Let all you speak and do show that you are little and base and mean and vile in your own eyes.

As one instance of this, be always ready to own any fault you have done. If you have at any time thought, spoken, or acted wrongly, do not be backward to acknowledge it. Never dream that this will hurt the cause of God. No, it will further it. Be therefore open and frank when you are taxed with anything. Do not seek either to evade or disguise it, but let it appear just as it is, and you will thereby not hinder but adorn the gospel.

Advice about Christian Unity

From *A Plain Account of Christian Perfection*

Wesley continues to quote from the 1762 tract (which he expands and edits to remove references to specific controversies—and individuals) with advice about Christian unity.

Beware of schism, of making a rent in the church of Christ. That inward disunion, the members ceasing to have a reciprocal love one for another, is the very root of all contention and every outward separation. Beware of everything tending thereto. Beware of a dividing spirit: shun whatever has the least aspect that way. Therefore, do not say, *"I belong to Paul or to Apollos,"* the very thing that occasioned the schism at Corinth. Do not say, "This is my preacher; the best preacher in England. Give me him, and take all the rest." All this tends to breed or foment division, to disunite those whom God has joined. Do not despise or run down any preacher; do not exalt any one above the rest lest you hurt both him and the cause of God. On the other hand, do not bear hard on any by reason of some incoherency or inaccuracy of expression, nor for some mistakes, were they really such.

Likewise, if you would avoid schism, observe every rule of the Society and of the bands for conscience's sake. Never omit meeting with your class or band. Never absent yourself from any public meeting. These are the very sinews of our Society; and whatever weakens, or tends to weaken, our regard for these, or our exactness in attending them, strikes at the very root of our community. As one says, "That part of our economy, the private weekly meetings for prayer, examination, and particular exhortation, has been the greatest means of deepening and confirming every blessing that was received by the word preached, and of diffusing it to others who could not attend the public ministry; whereas, without this religious connection and intercourse, the most ardent attempts by mere preaching have proved of no lasting use."

Do not allow yourself one thought of separating from your brothers and sisters, whether their opinions agree with yours or not. Do not dream that anyone sins in not believing you, in not taking your word; or that this or that opinion is essential to the work, and both must stand or fall together. Beware of any impatience of contradiction. Do not condemn or think harshly of those who cannot see just as you see, or who judge it their duty to contradict you, whether in a great thing or a small. I fear some of us have thought harshly of others merely because they contradicted what we affirmed. All this tends to division; and by everything of this kind we are teaching them an evil lesson against ourselves.

Oh, beware of touchiness, of testiness, not bearing to be spoken to; starting at the least word; and flying from those who do not implicitly receive my or another's sayings!

Expect contradiction and opposition, together with crosses of various kinds. Consider the words of Saint Paul: *He has graciously granted you the privilege*—for Christ's sake, as a fruit of his death and intercession for you—*not only of believing in Christ, but of suffering for him as well.* God gives you this opposition or reproach; it is a fresh token of his love. And will you disown the Giver, or spurn his gift, and count it a misfortune? Will you not rather say, *"Father, the hour has come for you to be glorified;* now you give your child to suffer something for you: do with me according to your will"? Know that these things, far from being hindrances to the work of God, or to your soul, unless by your own fault, are not only unavoidable in the course of Providence, but profitable, even necessary, for you. Therefore, receive them from God (not from chance) with willingness, with thankfulness. Receive them from people with humility, meekness, yieldingness, gentleness, sweetness. Why should not even your outward appearance and manner be soft? Remember the charity of Lady Cutts. It was said of the Roman Emperor Titus, never any one came displeased from him; but it might be said of her, never any one went displeased to her, so secure were all of the kind and favorable reception they would receive from her.

Beware of tempting others to separate from you. Give no offense that can possibly be avoided. See that your practice is in all things suitable to your profession, adorning the doctrine of God our Savior. Be particularly careful of speaking of yourself. You may not, indeed, deny the work of God. But speak of it, when you are called to do so, in the most inoffensive manner possible. Avoid all magnificent, pompous words. Indeed, you need give it no general name, neither perfection, sanctification, the second blessing, or the having attained. Rather speak of the particulars God has wrought for you. You may say, "At such a time I felt a change that I am not able to express; and since that time I have not felt pride, or self-will, or anger, or unbelief, nor anything but a fullness of love to God and to all humankind." And answer any other plain question that is asked with modesty and simplicity.

And if any of you should at any time fall from what you now are, if you should again feel pride or unbelief, or any temper from which you are now delivered—do not deny. Do not hide, do not disguise it at all, at the peril of your soul. At all events, go to one in whom you can confide, and speak just what you feel. God will enable that one to speak a word in season, which shall be health to your souls. And surely God will again lift up your head, and cause *the bones that have been crushed to rejoice.*

Advice about Growth in Grace

From *A Plain Account of Christian Perfection*

Wesley concludes the book with a series of reflections on the Christian life.

Most of the preceding advices are strongly enforced in the following reflections, which I recommend to your deep and frequent consideration, next to the Holy Scriptures.

(1) The sea is an excellent figure of the fullness of God, and that of the blessed Spirit. For as the rivers all return into the sea, so the bodies, the souls, and the good works of the righteous return into God, to live there in his eternal repose.

Although all the graces of God depend on his bounty, yet is he pleased generally to attach them to the prayers, the instructions, and the holiness of those with whom we are. By strong though invisible attractions God draws some souls through their intercourse with others.

The sympathies formed by grace far surpass those formed by nature.

The truly devout show that passions as naturally flow from true as from false love; so deeply sensible are they of the goods and evils of those they love for God's sake. But this can only be comprehended by those who understand the language of love.

The bottom of the soul may be in repose even while we are in many outward troubles, just as the bottom of the sea is calm, while the surface is strongly agitated.

The best helps to growth in grace are the ill usage, the affronts, and the losses that befall us. We should receive them with all thankfulness, as preferable to all others, were it only on this account: that our will has no part therein.

The readiest way to escape from our sufferings is to be willing that they should endure as long as God pleases.

If we bear persecution and affliction in a right manner, we attain a larger measure of conformity to Christ, by a due improvement of one of these occasions, than we could have done merely by imitating his mercy, in abundance of good works.

One of the greatest evidences of God's love to those who love him is to send them afflictions, with grace to bear them.

Even in the greatest afflictions, we ought to testify to God that in receiving them from his hand we feel pleasure in the midst of the pain from being afflicted by him who loved us, and whom we love.

The readiest way God takes to draw people to himself is to afflict them in what they love most and with good reason, and to cause this affliction to arise from some good action done with a single eye. Nothing can more clearly show them the emptiness of what is most lovely and desirable in the world.

(2) True resignation consists in a thorough conformity to the whole will of God, who wills and does all (excepting sin) that comes to pass in the world. In order to do this, we have only to embrace all events, good and bad, as God's will.

In the greatest afflictions that can befall the just, either from heaven or earth, they remain immovable in peace, and perfectly submissive to God by an inward, loving regard to him, uniting in one all the powers of their souls.

We ought quietly to accept whatever befalls us; to bear the defects of others and our own, to confess them to God in secret prayer, or with groans that cannot be uttered; but never to speak a sharp or peevish word, nor to murmur or repine; but thoroughly willing that God should treat you in the manner that pleases him. We are God's lambs and therefore ought to be ready to suffer, even to the death, without complaining.

We are to bear with those we cannot amend and to be content with offering them to God. This is true resignation. And since Christ has borne our infirmities, we may well bear those of each other for his sake.

To abandon all, to strip one's self of all in order to seek and to follow Jesus Christ naked to Bethlehem, where he was born; naked to the hall where he was scourged; and naked to Calvary, where he died on the cross, is so great a mercy that neither the thing nor the knowledge of it is given to any but through faith in the Son of God.

(3) There is no love of God without patience, and no patience without lowliness and sweetness of spirit.

Humility and patience are the surest proof of the increase of love.

Humility alone unites patience with love; without which it is impossible to draw profit from suffering, or indeed, to avoid complaint, especially when we think we have no occasion for what people make us suffer.

True humility is a kind of self-annihilation, and this is the center of all virtues.

Souls returned to God ought to be attentive to everything that is said to them, on the head of salvation, with a desire to profit thereby.

Of the sins that God has pardoned, let nothing remain but a deeper humility in the heart, and a stricter regulation in our words, in our actions, and in our sufferings.

(4) Putting up with people and bearing evils in meekness and silence is the sum of a Christian life.

God is the first object of our love. Its next office is to bear the defects of others. And we should begin the practice of this amidst our own household.

We should chiefly exercise our love toward them who most shock either our way of thinking, or our temper, or our knowledge, or the desire we have that others should be as virtuous as we wish to be ourselves.

(5) God hardly gives the Spirit even to those he has established in grace if they do not pray for it on all occasions, not only once, but many times.

God does nothing but in answer to prayer. Even those who have been converted to God without praying for it themselves (which is exceedingly rare), were not without the prayers of others. Every new victory that a soul gains is the effect of a new prayer.

On every occasion of uneasiness we should retire to prayer, that we may give place to the grace and light of God, and then form our resolutions, without being in any pain about what success they may have.

In the greatest temptations, a single look to Christ and barely pronouncing his name suffices to overcome the wicked one, if it be done with confidence and calmness of spirit.

God's command to *pray without ceasing* is founded on the necessity we have of God's grace to preserve the life of God in the soul, which can no more subsist one moment without it than the body can without air.

Whether we think of or speak to God, whether we act or suffer for him, all is prayer when we have no other object than his love and the desire of pleasing him.

All that Christians do, even in eating and sleeping, is prayer when done in simplicity, according to the order of God, without either adding to or diminishing from it by their own choice.

Prayer continues in the desire of the heart, though the understanding be employed on outward things.

In souls filled with love, the desire to please God is a continual prayer.

As the furious hate the devil bears toward us is termed the roaring of a lion, so our vehement love may be termed crying after God.

God only requires of his adult children that their hearts be truly purified and that they offer him continually the wishes and vows that naturally spring from perfect love. For these desires, being the genuine fruits of love, are the most perfect prayers that can spring from it.

Advice about Vigilance

From *A Plain Account of Christian Perfection*

The conclusion of Wesley's reflections on holy living.

(6) It is scarcely conceivable how narrow the way is wherein God leads those who follow him and how dependent on him we must be unless we are wanting in our faithfulness to him.

It is hardly believable of what great consequence before God the smallest things are, and what great inconveniences sometimes follow those that appear to be light faults.

As a very little dust will disorder a clock and the least sand will obscure our sight, so the least grain of sin that is upon the heart will hinder its right motion toward God.

We ought to be in the church as the saints are in heaven, and in the house as the holiest people are in the church: doing our work in the house as we pray in the church, worshiping God from the ground of the heart.

We should be continually laboring to cut off all the useless things that surround us. God usually removes the excesses of our souls in the same proportion as we do those of our bodies.

The best means of resisting the devil is to destroy whatever of the world remains in us in order to raise for God, upon its ruins, a building all of love. Then shall we begin, in this fleeting life, to love God as we shall love him in eternity.

We scarcely conceive how easy it is to rob God of his due in our friendship with the most virtuous persons until they are torn from us by death. But if this loss produce lasting sorrow, that is a clear proof that we had before two treasures, between which we divided our heart.

(7) If, after having renounced all, we do not watch incessantly and beseech God to accompany our vigilance with his, we shall be again entangled and overcome.

As the most dangerous winds may enter at little openings, so the devil never enters more dangerously than by little unobserved incidents, which seem to be nothing, yet insensibly open the heart to great temptations.

It is good to renew ourselves from time to time by closely examining the state of our souls, as if we had never done it before. For nothing tends more to the full assurance of faith than to keep ourselves by this means in humility and the exercise of all good works.

To continual watchfulness and prayer ought to be added continual employment. For grace flies in a vacuum as well as nature, and the devil fills whatever God does not fill.

There is no faithfulness like that which ought to be between a guide of souls and the person directed by that one. They ought continually to regard each other in God and closely to examine themselves, whether all their thoughts are pure and all their words directed with Christian discretion. Other affairs are only the things of people. But these are peculiarly the things of God.

(8) The words of Saint Paul, *no one can say "Jesus is Lord" except by the Holy Spirit,* show us the necessity of eyeing God in our good works and even in our minutest thoughts. We know that none are pleasing to God but those that he forms in us and with us. From hence we learn that we cannot serve God unless God use our tongue, hands, and heart to do by himself and his Spirit whatever he would have us to do.

If we were not utterly impotent, our good works would be our own property; whereas now they belong wholly to God, because they proceed from God and God's grace. While raising our works, and making them all divine, God honors himself in us through them.

One of the principal rules of religion is to lose no occasion for serving God. And since God is invisible to our eyes, we are to serve God in our neighbor, which God receives as if done to himself in person, standing visibly before us.

God does not love people who are inconstant nor good works that are intermittent. Nothing is pleasing to God but what has a resemblance of God's own immutability.

A constant attention to the work God entrusts us with is a mark of solid piety.

Love fasts when it can, and as much as it can. It leads to all the ordinances of God and employs itself in all the outward works whereof it is capable. It flies, as it were, like Elijah over the plain, to find God upon the holy mountain.

God is so great that he communicates greatness to the least thing that is done for his service.

Happy are they who are sick, or even lose their life for having done a good work.

God frequently conceals the part his children have in the conversion of other souls. Yet one may boldly say that the person who long groans before God for the conversion of another, whenever that soul is converted to God, is one of the chief causes of it.

Charity cannot be practiced right, unless, first, we exercise it the moment God gives the occasion; and, second, retire the instant after to offer it to God by humble thanksgiving. And this for three reasons—first, to render God what we have received from him. Second, to avoid the dangerous temptation that springs from the very goodness of these works. And third, to unite ourselves to God, in whom the soul expands itself in prayer with all the graces we have received and the good works we have done. So we draw from God new strength against the bad effects that these very works may produce in us, if we do not make use of the antidotes that God has ordained against these poisons. The true means to be filled anew with the riches of grace is thus to strip ourselves of it. Without this it is extremely difficult not to grow faint in the practice of good works.

Good works do not receive their last perfection till they, as it were, lose themselves in God. This is a kind of death to them, resembling that of our bodies, which will not attain their highest life, their immortality, till they lose themselves in the glory of our souls, or rather of God, wherewith they shall be filled. And it is only what they had of the earthly and mortal that good works lose by this spiritual death.

Fire is the symbol of love. And the love of God is the principle and the end of all our good works. But the truth surpasses the symbol, and the fire of divine love has this advantage over material fire, that it can reascend to its source, and raise to these with it all the good works that it produces. And by this means it prevents their being corrupted by pride, vanity, or any evil mixture. But this cannot be done otherwise than by making these good works in a spiritual manner die in God, by a deep gratitude, which plunges the soul in God as in an abyss, with all that it is, and all the grace and works for which it is indebted to him. By this gratitude the soul seems to empty itself of them, that they may return to their source, as rivers seem willing to empty themselves when they pour themselves with all their waters into the sea.

When we have received any favor from God, we ought to retire, if not into our closets, into our hearts, and say, "I come,

Lord, to restore to you what you have given. I freely relinquish it, to enter again into my own nothingness. For what is the most perfect creature in heaven or earth in your presence, but a void capable of being filled with you and by you as the air that is void and dark is capable of being filled with the light of the sun, who withdraws it every day to restore it the next, there being nothing in the air that either appropriates this light or resists it? Oh, give me the same facility of receiving and restoring your grace and good works! I say 'your,' for I acknowledge the root from which they spring is in you, and not in me."

Appendix

Reading Spiritual Classics for Personal and Group Formation

Many Christians today are searching for more spiritual depth, for something more than simply being good church members. That quest may send them to the spiritual practices of New Age movements or of Eastern religions such as Zen Buddhism. Christians, though, have their own long spiritual tradition, a tradition rich with wisdom, variety, and depth.

The great spiritual classics testify to that depth. They do not concern themselves with mystical flights for a spiritual elite. Rather, they contain very practical advice and insights that can support and shape the spiritual growth of any Christian. We can all benefit by sitting at the feet of the masters (both male and female) of Christian spirituality.

Reading spiritual classics is different from most of the reading we do. We have learned to read to master a text and extract information from it. We tend to read quickly, to get through a text. And we summarize as we read, seeking the main point. In reading spiritual classics, though, we allow the text to master and form us. Such formative reading goes more slowly, more reflectively, allowing time for God to speak to us through the text. God's word for us may come as easily from a minor point or even an aside as from the major point.

Formative reading requires that you approach the text in humility. Read as a seeker, not as an expert. Don't demand that the text meet your expectations for what an "enlightened" author should write. Humility means accepting the author as another imperfect human, a product of his or her own time and situation. Learn to celebrate what is foundational in an author's writing without being overly disturbed by what is peculiar to the author's life and times. Trust the text as a gift from both God and the author, offered to you for your benefit—to help you grow in Christ.

To read formatively, you must also slow down. Feel free to reread a passage that seems to speak specially to you. Stop from time to time to reflect on what you have been reading. Keep a journal for these reflections. Often the act of writing can itself prompt further, deeper reflection. Keep your notebook open and your pencil in hand as you read. You might not get back to that wonderful insight later. Don't worry that you are not getting through an entire passage—or even the first paragraph! Formative reading is about depth rather than breadth, quality rather than quantity. As you read, seek God's direction for your own life. Timeless truths have their place but may not be what is most important for your own formation here and now.

As you read the passage, you might keep some of these questions running through your mind:

- How is what I'm reading true of my own life? Where does it reflect my own *experience?*
- How does this text challenge me? What new *direction* does it offer me?
- What must I change to put what I am reading into practice? How can I *incarnate* it, let this word become flesh in my life?

You might also devote special attention to sections that upset you. What is the source of the disturbance? Do you want to argue theology? Are you turned off by cultural differences? Or have you been skewered by an insight that would turn your life upside down if you took it seriously? Let your journal be a dialogue with the text.

If you find yourself moving from reading the text to chewing over its implications to praying, that's great! Spiritual reading is really the first step in an ancient way of prayer called *lectio divina* or "divine reading." Reading leads naturally into reflection on what you have read (meditation). As you reflect on what the text might mean for your life, you may well want to ask for God's help in living out any new insights or direction you have perceived (prayer). Sometimes such prayer may lead you further into silently abiding in God's presence (contemplation). And, of course, the process is only really completed when it begins to make a difference in the way we live (incarnation).

As good as it is to read spiritual classics in solitude, it is even better to join with others in a small group for mutual formation or "spiritual direction in common." This is *not* the same as a study group that talks *about* spiritual classics. A group for mutual formation would have similar goals as for an individual's reading: to allow the text to shine its light on the *experiences* of the group members, to suggest new *directions* for their lives and practical ways of *incarnating* these directions. Such a group might agree to focus on one short passage from a classic at each meeting (even if members have read more). Discussion usually goes much deeper if all the members have already read and reflected on the passage before the meeting and bring their journals.

Such groups need to watch for several potential problems. It is easy to go off on a tangent (especially if it takes the focus off the members' own experience and onto generalities). At such times a group leader might bring the group's attention back to the text: "What does our author say about that?" Or, "How do we experience that in our own lives?" When a group member shares a problem, others may be tempted to try to "fix" it. This is much less helpful than sharing similar experiences and how they were handled (for good or ill). "Sharing" someone else's problems (whether that person is in or out of the group) should be strongly discouraged.

One person could be designated as leader, to be responsible for opening and closing prayers; to be the first to share or respond to the text; and to keep notes during the discussion to highlight recurring themes, challenges, directives, or practical steps. These responsibilities could also be shared among several members of the group or rotated.

For further information about formative reading of spiritual classics, try *A Practical Guide to Spiritual Reading* by Susan Annette Muto. *Shaped by the Word: The Power of Scripture in Spiritual Formation* by M. Robert Mulholland Jr. covers formative reading of the Bible. *Good Things Happen: Experiencing Community in Small Groups* by Dick Westley is an excellent resource on forming small groups of all kinds.

CPSIA information can be obtained
at www.ICGtesting.com
Printed in the USA
FSOW04n0233180417
33246FS